Home Office Research Study 252

Crime prevention effects of closed circuit television: a systematic review

Brandon C. Welsh and David P. Farrington

The views expressed in this report are those of the authors, not necessarily those of the Home Office (nor do they reflect Government policy).

Home Office Research, Development and Statistics Directorate
August 2002

Home Office Research Studies

The Home Office Research Studies are reports on research undertaken by or on behalf of the Home Office. They cover the range of subjects for which the Home Secretary has responsibility. Other publications produced by the Research, Development and Statistics Directorate include Findings, Statistical Bulletins and Statistical Papers.

The Research, Development and Statistics Directorate

RDS is part of the Home Office. The Home Office's purpose is to build a safe, just and tolerant society in which the rights and responsibilities of individuals, families and communities are properly balanced and the protection and security of the public are maintained.

RDS is also part of National Statistics (NS). One of the aims of NS is to inform Parliament and the citizen about the state of the nation and provide a window on the work and performance of government, allowing the impact of government policies and actions to be assessed.

Therefore –

Research Development and Statistics Directorate exists to improve policy making, decision taking and practice in support of the Home Office purpose and aims, to provide the public and Parliament with information necessary for informed debate and to publish information for future use.

First published 2002
Application for reproduction should be made to the Communication Development Unit, Room 201, Home Office, 50 Queen Anne's Gate, London SW1H 9AT.

Foreword

This review summarises the findings of previous studies from both the USA and Britain on the effectiveness of CCTV in crime reduction. Forty six relevant studies were assessed according to strict methodological criteria:

that CCTV was the main intervention studied;
that there was an outcome measure of crime;
that crime levels before and after the intervention were measured;
that the studies included a comparable control area.

The authors considered only 22 of these surveys to be rigorous enough for inclusion in their meta-analysis. The review draws conclusions on the effectiveness of CCTV generally and on its effectiveness in terms of specific settings (e.g. car parks, public transport or city centres).

Overall, the best current evidence suggests that CCTV reduces crime to a small degree. CCTV is most effective in reducing vehicle crime in car parks, but it had little or no effect on crime in public transport and city centre settings.

Importantly, the review draws attention to the shortcomings of many of the previous evaluations and highlights common methodological problems that either resulted in their exclusion from the review or in their limited value in the debate.

The review includes a useful summary of the knowledge gaps in relation to the impact of CCTV on crime and sets out the key elements needed in future research and evaluation if these questions are to be addressed.

Carole F Willis
Head of Policing and Reducing Crime Unit

Acknowledgements

We thank Hugh Arnold, London Borough of Sutton; Professor Trevor Bennett, University of Glamorgan; Professor Jason Ditton, University of Sheffield and Scottish Centre for Criminology; Professor John E. Eck, University of Cincinnati; Professor Lorraine Mazerolle, Griffith University; Professor Sara McLafferty, Hunter College; David Skinns, Doncaster College; Dr Peter Squires, University of Brighton; and Professor Pierre Tremblay, University of Montreal, for providing helpful assistance in obtaining copies of evaluation studies used in this report. Appreciation is also extended to Professor Nick Tilley, Nottingham Trent University, for comments on the proposal for this research; Deborah Friedman, University of Massachusetts Lowell, for help with the collection of reports; Jennifer Wylie, for translation services; and Professor Martin Gill, Leicester University, for helpful comments on the report. Thanks also go to Professor Ross Homel, Griffith University, Australia and Professor Graham Farrell, University of Cincinnati, USA, for acting as independent assessors for this report.

Brandon C. Welsh
David P. Farrington

Brandon C. Welsh is an Assistant Professor in the Department of Criminal Justice, University of Massachusetts Lowell. David P. Farrington is Professor of Psychological Criminology in the Institute of Criminology, University of Cambridge.

Contents

List of Tables

List of Figures

Summary

Closed circuit television serves many functions and is used in both public and private settings. The prevention of crime (i.e., personal and property) is among its primary objectives in public space. This report aims to evaluate the evidence on the effectiveness of CCTV in preventing crime.

Determining what works to reduce crime requires examination of the results of prior evaluation studies. This is better than drawing conclusions about what works from personal experience, from anecdotal evidence, from widespread beliefs, or from a single study which was well-funded or highly publicised. This is the foundation of an evidence-based approach to preventing crime, and the systematic review represents an innovative, scientific method for contributing to evidence-based prevention of crime.

This report has two main objectives: (1) to report on the findings of a systematic review – incorporating meta-analytic techniques – of the available research evidence on the effects of CCTV on crime, and (2) to inform public policy and practice on preventing crime through the use of CCTV interventions.

Systematic reviews use rigorous methods for locating, appraising, and synthesising evidence from prior evaluation studies, and they are reported with the same level of detail that characterises high quality reports of original research.

Evaluations meeting the following criteria were included in this review:
  (1) CCTV was the focus of the intervention
  (2) there was an outcome measure of crime
  (3) the evaluation design was of high methodological quality, with the minimum design involving before-and-after measures of crime in experimental and control areas
  (4) there was at least one experimental area and one comparable control area
  (5) the total number of crimes in each area before the intervention was at least 20.

The following four search strategies were carried out to identify CCTV evaluations meeting the criteria for inclusion in this review:
  (1) searches of on-line databases
  (2) searches of reviews of the literature on the effectiveness of CCTV in preventing crime
  (3) searches of bibliographies of CCTV reports
  (4) contacts with leading researchers.

Both published and unpublished reports were considered in the searches, and the searches were international in scope and were not limited to the English language.

The search strategies resulted in 22 CCTV evaluations meeting the criteria for inclusion. The evaluations were carried out in three main settings: (1) city centre or public housing, (2) public transport, and (3) car parks.

Of the 22 included evaluations, half (11) found a desirable effect on crime and five found an undesirable effect on crime. Five evaluations found a null effect on crime (i.e., clear evidence of no effect), while the remaining one was classified as finding an uncertain effect on crime (i.e., unclear evidence of an effect).

Results from a meta-analysis provide a clearer picture of the crime prevention effectiveness of CCTV. From 18 evaluations – the other four did not provide the needed data to be included in the meta-analysis – it was concluded that CCTV had a significant desirable effect on crime, although the overall reduction in crime was a very small four per cent. Half of the studies (nine out of 18) showed evidence of a desirable effect of CCTV on crime. All nine of these studies were carried out in the UK. Conversely, the other nine studies showed no evidence of any desirable effect of CCTV on crime. All five North American studies were in this group.

The meta-analysis also examined the effect of CCTV on the most frequently measured crime types. It was found that CCTV had no effect on violent crimes (from five studies), but had a significant desirable effect on vehicle crimes (from eight studies).

Across the three settings, mixed results were found for the crime prevention effectiveness of CCTV. In the city centre and public housing setting, there was evidence that CCTV led to a negligible reduction in crime of about two per cent in experimental areas compared with control areas. CCTV had a very small but significant effect on crime in the five UK evaluations in this setting (three desirable and two undesirable), but had no effect on crime in the four North American evaluations.

The four evaluations of CCTV in public transportation systems present conflicting evidence of effectiveness: two found a desirable effect, one found no effect, and one found an undesirable effect on crime. For the two effective studies, the use of other interventions makes it difficult to say with certainty that CCTV produced the observed crime reductions. The pooled effect size for all four studies was a non-significant six per cent decrease in crime.

In car parks, there was evidence that CCTV led to a statistically significant reduction in crime of about 41 per cent in experimental areas compared with control areas. For all of the studies in this setting other measures were in operation at the same time as CCTV.

Advancing knowledge about the crime prevention benefits of CCTV schemes should begin with attention to the methodological rigour of the evaluation designs. The use of a control condition is important in ruling out some of the major threats to internal validity, but efforts are also needed to make the experimental and control conditions comparable. Attention to methodological problems or changes to programmes that take place during and after implementation is needed. Statistical power analysis is needed in advance to determine if numbers are sufficient to detect the strength of likely effects. There is also the need for longer follow-up periods to see how far effects persist. Research is needed to help identify the active ingredients and causal mechanisms of successful CCTV programmes and future experiments are needed which attempt to disentangle elements of effective programmes. Research is also needed on the financial costs and benefits of CCTV programmes. Future evaluations need to include alternative methods of measuring crime (surveys as well as police records).

The studies included in the present review show that CCTV can be most effective in reducing crime in car parks. Exactly what are the optimal circumstances for effective use of CCTV schemes is not entirely clear at present, and needs to be established by future evaluation research. Interestingly, the success of the CCTV schemes in car parks was limited to a reduction in vehicle crimes (the only crime type measured) and all five schemes included other interventions, such as improved lighting and notices about CCTV cameras. Conversely, the evaluations of CCTV schemes in city centres and public housing measured a much larger range of crime types and the schemes did not involve, with one exception, other interventions. These CCTV schemes, and those focused on public transport, had only a small effect on crime. Could it be that a package of interventions focused on a specific crime type is what made the CCTV-led schemes in car parks effective?

Overall, it might be concluded that CCTV reduces crime to a small degree. Future CCTV schemes should be carefully implemented in different settings and should employ high quality evaluation designs with long follow-up periods. In the end, an evidence-based approach to crime prevention which uses the highest level of science available offers the strongest formula for building a safer society.

1. Background

Closed circuit television serves many functions and is used in both public and private settings. The prevention of crime (i.e., personal and property) is among its primary objectives in public space, and this is the focus of the present report.

As an intervention targeted at crime, CCTV is a type of situational crime prevention (e.g., Clarke, 1995). According to Clarke and Homel's (1997) classification of situational crime prevention, CCTV is viewed as a technique of "formal surveillance". In this regard, CCTV cameras are seen to enhance or take the place of security personnel.

The mechanisms by which CCTV may prevent crime are numerous. These have been articulated by Armitage and her colleagues (1999, pp. 226-27), and are as follows:

- *Caught in the act* – perpetrators will be detected, and possibly removed or deterred.

- *You've been framed* – CCTV deters potential offenders who perceive an elevated risk of apprehension.

- *Nosy parker* – CCTV may lead more people to feel able to frequent the surveilled places. This will increase the extent of natural surveillance by newcomers, which may deter potential offenders.

- *Effective deployment* – CCTV directs security personnel to ambiguous situations, which may head off their translation into crime.

- *Publicity* – CCTV could symbolise efforts to take crime seriously, and the perception of those efforts may both energise law-abiding citizens and/or deter crime.

- *Time for crime* – CCTV may be perceived as reducing the time available to commit crime, preventing those crimes that require extended time and effort.

- *Memory jogging* – the presence of CCTV may induce people to take elementary security precautions, such as locking their car, by jogging their memory.

- *Anticipated shaming* – the presence of CCTV may induce people to take elementary security precautions, for fear that they will be shamed by being shown on CCTV.

- *Appeal to the cautious* – cautious people migrate to the areas with CCTV to shop, leave their cars, and so on. Their caution and security-mindedness reduce the risk.

- *Reporting changes* – people report (and/or police record) fewer of the crimes that occur, either because they wish to show the [desirable] effects of CCTV or out of a belief that "the Council is doing its best" and nothing should be done to discourage it.

The growth in the use of CCTV to prevent crime in recent years, especially in the United Kingdom (Norris and Armstrong, 1999) and, surprisingly to a much lesser extent, in the United States (Nieto, 1997), and the increased attention to research on evaluating its effectiveness against crime (Eck, 1997, 2002; Phillips, 1999), were important reasons for carrying out the present research.

Determining what works to reduce crime requires us to examine the results of prior evaluation studies. This is better than drawing conclusions about what works from personal experience, from anecdotal evidence, from widespread beliefs, or from a single study which was well-funded or highly publicised. This is the foundation of an evidence-based approach to preventing crime, and the systematic review (see below), which serves as the basis of this report, represents an innovative, scientific method for contributing to evidence-based prevention of crime.

This report has two main objectives: (1) to report on the findings of a systematic review – incorporating meta-analytic techniques – of the available research evidence on the effects of CCTV on crime, and (2) to inform public policy and practice on preventing crime through the use of CCTV interventions.

This report is divided into four chapters. The second chapter reports on the criteria for inclusion of CCTV evaluations in this review and the methods used to search for, code, and analyse evaluation reports of CCTV programmes. The third chapter discusses the research findings organised by the setting in which CCTV evaluations were conducted, and the final chapter summarises the main findings and identifies priorities for future research and policy implications.

2.   Method

The present report presents a systematic review of the effects of CCTV on crime and follows closely the methodology of this review technique. Systematic reviews use rigorous methods for locating, appraising and synthesising evidence from prior evaluation studies, and they are reported with the same level of detail that characterises high quality reports of original research. According to Johnson *et al.* (2000, p. 35), systematic reviews "essentially take an epidemiological look at the methodology and results sections of a specific population of studies to reach a research-based consensus on a given study topic". They have explicit objectives, explicit criteria for including or excluding studies, extensive searches for eligible evaluation studies from all over the world, careful extraction and coding of key features of studies, and a structured and detailed report of the methods and conclusions of the review. All of this contributes greatly to the ease of their interpretation and replication by other researchers. It is beyond the scope of this report to discuss all of the features of systematic reviews, but interested readers should consult key reports on the topic (see e.g., Farrington and Petrosino, 2000; Johnson *et al.*, 2000; Farrington and Welsh, 2001; Farrington *et al.*, 2001).

Criteria for inclusion of evaluation studies

In selecting evaluations for inclusion in this review, the following criteria were used:

(1) CCTV was the focus of the intervention. For evaluations involving one or more other interventions, only those evaluations in which CCTV was the main intervention were included. The determination of the main intervention was based on the author identifying it as such or, if the author did not do this, the importance of CCTV relative to the other interventions. For a small number of included evaluations with multiple interventions, the main intervention was not identified, but it was clear from the report that CCTV was the most important intervention. It is desirable to include only evaluations where CCTV was the main intervention, because in other cases it is impossible to disentangle the effects of CCTV from the effects of other interventions.

(2) There was an outcome measure of crime. The most relevant crime outcomes were violent and property crimes (especially vehicle crimes).

(3) The evaluation design was of high methodological quality, with the minimum design involving before-and-after measures of crime in experimental and control areas. The unit of interest is the area (including car parks and underground stations).

(4) There was at least one experimental area and one comparable control area. Studies involving residential, business or commercial areas (e.g., city centres), and other public and private areas (e.g., underground stations, car parks) were eligible for inclusion. Studies that compared an experimental area with the remainder of a city were excluded, because the control area was non-comparable.

(5) The total number of crimes in each area before the intervention was at least 20. The main measure of effect size was based on changes in crime rates between the before and after time periods. It was considered that a measure of change based on an N below 20 was potentially misleading. Also, any study with fewer than 20 crimes before would have insufficient statistical power to detect changes in crime. The criterion of 20 is probably too low, but we were reluctant to exclude studies unless their numbers were clearly inadequate.

It is worth saying a few more words about criterion 3. Ideally, the "gold standard" of the randomised experiment, which is the most convincing method of evaluating crime prevention programmes (Farrington, 1983), would have been used. The key feature of randomised controlled trials, which are widely used in medical evaluations, is that the experimental and control groups are equated before the experimental intervention on all possible extraneous variables. Hence, any subsequent differences between them must be attributable to the intervention. Technically, randomised experiments have the highest possible internal validity in unambiguously attributing an effect to a cause (Shadish et al., 2002).

The randomised experiment, however, is only the most convincing method of evaluation if a sufficiently large number of units is randomly assigned to ensure that the experimental group is equivalent to the control group on all possible extraneous variables (within the limits of statistical fluctuation). As a rule of thumb, at least 50 units in each category are needed. This number is relatively easy to achieve with individuals but very difficult to achieve with larger units such as areas, as in the evaluation of CCTV schemes. For larger units such as areas, the best and most feasible design usually involves before-and-after measures in experimental and control conditions together with statistical control of extraneous variables (Farrington, 1997). The use of a control condition that is comparable with the experimental condition is necessary in order to exclude threats to internal validity.

Search strategies

The following four search strategies were carried out to identify CCTV evaluations meeting the criteria for inclusion in this review:
  (1) searches of on-line databases (see below)
  (2) searches of reviews of the literature on the effectiveness of CCTV in preventing crime (for a list of reviews consulted, see Appendix 1)
  (3) searches of bibliographies of CCTV reports
  (4) contacts with leading researchers (see Acknowledgements).

Both published and unpublished reports were included in the searches. Furthermore, the searches were international in scope and were not limited to the English language (one non-English language evaluation report is included in the review). Searches (1) through (3) were completed in January 2001 and reflect material published or known up to 31 December 2000.

The following eight databases were searched:
  (1) Criminal Justice Abstracts
  (2) National Criminal Justice Reference Service (NCJRS) Abstracts
  (3) Sociological Abstracts
  (4) Social Science Abstracts (SocialSciAbs)
  (5) Educational Resources Information Clearinghouse (ERIC)
  (6) Government Publications Office Monthly Catalog (GPO Monthly)
  (7) Psychology Information (PsychInfo)
  (8) Public Affairs Information Service (PAIS) International

These databases were selected because they had the most comprehensive coverage of criminological, criminal justice, and social science literatures. They are also among the top databases recommended by the Crime and Justice Group of the Campbell Collaboration, and other systematic reviews of interventions in the field of crime and justice have used them (e.g., Petrosino, 2000; Petrosino *et al.*, 2000).

The following terms were used to search the eight databases noted above: closed circuit television, CCTV, cameras, social control, surveillance, and formal surveillance. When applicable, "crime" was then added to each of these terms (e.g., CCTV and crime) to narrow the search parameters.

These search strategies resulted in the collection of 22 CCTV evaluations meeting the criteria for inclusion in this review. A few of the evaluations identified, which may or may not have met the criteria for inclusion, could not be obtained. The reports of these evaluations are listed in Appendix 2.

Key features of evaluations

Tables 3.1, 3.3, and 3.5 summarise key features of the 22 included CCTV evaluations.

- *Author, publication date, and location.* The authors and dates of the most relevant evaluation reports are listed here, along with the location of the programme. The evaluations have been listed in chronological order, according to the date of publication.

- *Context of intervention.* This is defined as the physical setting in which the CCTV intervention took place.

- *Type and duration of intervention.* The intervention is identified and any key features are listed. The length of time the programme was in operation is also noted here.

- *Sample size.* The number and any special features of the experimental and control areas are identified.

- *Other interventions.* Interventions other than CCTV which were employed at the time of the programme are identified.

- *Outcome measure of interest and data source.* As noted above, crime was the outcome measure of interest to this review. Here the specific crime types as well as the data source of the outcome measure are identified.

- *Research design and before-after time period.* As noted above, the minimum research design for an evaluation to be included in this review involves before-and-after measures of crime in comparable experimental and control areas. If matching or other statistical analysis techniques were used as part of the evaluation of programme effects, these too are noted here. The before and after time periods of the evaluation are also noted.

- *Results.* In summarising results, the focus was on the most relevant crime outcomes for this review (i.e., property and violent crime types) and comparisons between experimental and control areas. The results of significance tests are listed, but they were rarely provided by researchers. Similarly, few effect size measures were provided. The problem with significance tests is that they depend partly on sample size and partly on strength of effect. A significant result in a large sample could correspond to a rather small effect size, and conversely a large effect size in a small sample may not be statistically significant. Consequently, this report relies on measures of effect size (and associated confidence intervals) where possible.

Each of the evaluations were rated on their effectiveness in reducing crime. Each evaluation is assigned to one of the following four categories:
  (1) desirable effect: significant decrease in crime
  (2) undesirable effect: significant increase in crime
  (3) null effect: clear evidence of no effect on crime
  (4) uncertain effect: unclear evidence of an effect on crime.

Category 4 was assigned to those evaluations in which methodological problems (i.e., small numbers of crimes or contamination of control areas) confounded the reported results to the point that the evaluation could not be assigned to one of the other three categories. It was difficult to rate those evaluations which reported the percentage change in crime (from before to after the programme was implemented), but did not provide data on the number of crimes in the before and after periods. Instead of giving these evaluations a rating of "uncertain effect", they were rated subjectively on the basis of the reported percentage change in crime.

- *Other dimensions.* CCTV evaluations differ on many different dimensions, and it is impossible to include more than a few in summary tables. Two important issues that are addressed, not in the tables, but in the accompanying text, are displacement and diffusion of benefits. Displacement is often defined as the unintended increase in targeted crimes in other locations following from the introduction of a crime reduction scheme (for a discussion of "benign" or desirable effects of displacement, see Barr and Pease, 1990). Five different forms of displacement have been identified by Reppetto (1976): temporal (change in time), tactical (change in method), target (change in victim), territorial (change in place), and functional (change in type of crime). Diffusion of benefits is defined as the unintended decrease in non-targeted crimes following from a crime reduction scheme, or the "complete reverse" of displacement (Clarke and Weisburd, 1994).

In order to investigate territorial displacement and diffusion of benefits, the minimum design involves one experimental area, one adjacent area, and one non-adjacent control area. If crime decreased in the experimental area, increased in the adjacent area, and stayed constant in the control area, this might be evidence of displacement. If crime decreased in the experimental and adjacent areas and stayed constant or increased in the control area, this might be evidence of diffusion of benefits. Very few of the included evaluations had both adjacent and non-adjacent but comparable control areas. More had an adjacent control area and the remainder of the city as another control area, for example.

Evaluations not meeting inclusion criteria

When coding CCTV evaluations, many did not meet the criteria for inclusion and thus have not been included in the present review. Altogether, 24 CCTV evaluations were excluded. Table 2.1 lists these evaluations, summarises their key features, and identifies the reasons for exclusion. The reasons for discussing these evaluations here are two-fold: first, it conforms with the widely-held practice in systematic reviews of listing excluded studies and second, it allows readers to judge for themselves the strength of observed effects in excluded evaluations compared with those included.

As shown in Table 2.1, 17 of the 24 evaluations were excluded because no control area was used in evaluating the impact of the intervention. Another four evaluations were excluded because no comparable control area was used. The remaining three evaluations (King's Lynn, in Brown, 1995; Squires, 1998b, d) were excluded because they did not report crime data. Missing information on the few key features listed in Table 2.1 was not much of a problem with the 24 evaluations, although three failed to specify the length of the follow-up period. For the 21 evaluations that did provide information on the follow-up period, nine involved follow-ups of less than one year. Many of the CCTV schemes appeared to be successful in reducing a range of crimes, including robbery, assault, burglary, motor vehicle theft and vandalism. However, a number of the evaluations of these schemes were limited by small numbers of crimes. Because of methodological problems it is difficult to give much credence to the results of these evaluations.

Table 2.1: *CCTV evaluations not meeting inclusion criteria*

Author, publication date, and location	Reason for not including programme	Other interventions	Sample size	Follow-up and results
Burrows (1991)	No control area	Changes in store design and procedures	1 store (Tesco – large retailer)	n.a.; "unknown losses": approx. £12,000 to £5,000 per week; cash losses (from tills): approx. £500 to £20 per week
National Association of Convenience Stores, multiple sites, (1991), USA	No control area	n.a.	189 convenience stores	2 years; robbery: -15.2% (1.58 to 1.34 per store per year, NS)
Poyner (1992), North Shields	No control area	Media publicity and school visits	5 buses	8 months; vandalism: -52.9% (51 to 24)
Carr and Spring (1993), Victoria, Australia	No control area	Multiple (e.g., improved lighting, police)	Train, tram, and bus systems of Public Transport System	2 years; crimes against persons: -42.2% (57.3 to 33.1 per month); vandalism: -83.6% (700 to 115 broken windows, weekly average)
Tilley (1993a), Salford	No control area	None	3 businesses	12 months; total crimes: -14.3% (35 to 30)
1. Tilley (1993b), Lewisham	No control area	Media publicity and notices of CCTV	1 station car park	4 months; vehicle crimes: -75.0% (24 to 6)
2. Tilley (1993b), Hull	No comparable control area	None	E=1 car park, C=city centre as a whole	8 months; E vs C: theft of vehicles: -88.9% (27 to 3) vs -5.6% (430 to 406); theft from vehicles: -76.3% (38 to 9) vs +2.8% (961 to 988)

Author, publication date, and location	Reason for not including programme	Other interventions	Sample size	Follow-up and results
3. Tilley (1993b), Wolverhampton	No comparable control area	Notices of CCTV	E=1 car park, C=subdivision as a whole	13 months; E vs C: theft of vehicles: -18.2% (11 to 9) vs +3% (data n.a.); theft from vehicles: -46.4% (28 to 15) vs -3% (data n.a.)
Chatterton and Frenz (1994), Merseyside	No control area	Notices of CCTV	15 housing schemes ("sheltered accommodation")	5-10 months; burglary (completions and attempts): -78.8% (4.25 to 0.9 per month)[a]
Davidson and Farr (1994), Mitchelhill Estate, Glasgow	No control area	Multiple (e.g., target hardening, local management)	5 housing blocks	15 months; total crime[b]: -63.1% (28.7 to 10.6 average per quarter year)
Brown (1995), King's Lynn	No crime data for experimental or control areas	None	E=car parks and adjacent streets, C=rest of police division	32 months; E vs C: theft of vehicles: decline (data n.a.) vs ? (data n.a.); theft from vehicles: decline (data n.a.) vs decline (data n.a.); burglary (data n.a.) vs ? (data n.a.)
Squires and Measor (1996), Brighton	No comparable control area	None	E=police beats 1-4, C=rest of Brighton	12 months; E vs C: total crimes: "under" -10% (data n.a.) vs -1% (data n.a.)
Bromley and Thomas (1997), Cardiff and Swansea	No control area	Multiple (e.g., staff at exits, painting)	Different types of car parks	n.a. (no before measures); vehicle crimes: Cardiff (8.3/100 spaces) vs. Swansea (13.7/100 spaces)
Gill and Turbin (1998, 1999), Leeds and Sheffield	No control area	None	2 retail stores	n.a.; stock losses from theft (before-during phases and Leeds store only): £600 to £200 per week

Study	Control area		Areas	Results
Squires (1998b), Burgess Hill	No crime data for control area	None	E=town centre (beat 1), C=beat 1 excluding surveillance area	8 months; E vs C: total crime: -37.2% (data n.a.) vs ? (data n.a.)
Squires (1998c), Crawley	No comparable control area	None	E1=town centre (beat 1), E2=E1 + 3 shopping parades; C=rest of Crawley	6 months; E1 vs C: total crimes: -12% (data n.a.) vs -3% (data n.a.)
Squires (1998d), East Grinstead	No crime data for control area	None	E=town centre (beat 1), C=beat 1 excluding surveillance area	8 months; E vs C: total crime: -25.6% (data n.a.) vs ? (data n.a.)
Beck and Willis (1999), multiple sites	No control area	None	15 stores: E1=3 high level system; E2=6 medium level, E3= 6 low level	6 months; theft (by staff and customers):[c] E1=+37.8% (1.96% to 2.70%), E2=-17.9% (2.40% to 1.97%) E3=-26.6% (2.63% to 1.93%)
Ditton and Short (1999) and Ditton et al. (1999), Glasgow	No control area	None	28 police beats in city centre	12 months; total crimes: +9% (data n.a.)
1. Sivarajasingam and Shepherd (1999), Cardiff	No control area	None	1 city centre or town area	2 years; A&E recorded assault: -11.5% (7,066 to 6,251); police-recorded assault: +20.8% (677 to 818)
2. Sivarajasingam and Shepherd (1999), Swansea	No control area	None	1 city centre or town area	2 years; A&E recorded assault: +3.0% (3,967 to 4,086); police-recorded assault: -34.0% (486 to 321)

Author, publication date, and location	Reason for not including programme	Other interventions	Sample size	Follow-up and results
3. Sivarajasingam and Shepherd (1999), Rhyl	No control area	None	1 city centre or town area (1,249 assault: -24.0% (526 to 400)	2 years; A&E recorded assault: +46.0% (1,823); police-recorded
1. Taylor (1999), Leicester (West End)	No control area	Multiple (e.g., silent alarm)	154 businesses (data n.a.)	11 months; commercial burglary: decline
2. Taylor (1999), Leicester (Belgrave)	No control area	Multiple (e.g., silent alarm)	n.a.	24 months; commercial burglary: decline (data n.a.)

a   The total number of offences were 51 in the before period and 9 in the after period. "In 13 of the 15 schemes, no offenses of burglary were recorded for the period after CCTV was installed. One scheme had no burglaries in either period, and in another, there was a slight increase after camera installation" (Chatterton and Frenz, 1994, p. 136).

b   The individual crimes and their before-after comparisons (average per quarter year) were as follows: burglary (19.0 to 5.4), theft of and from vehicles (4.7 to 1.4), theft other (2.0 to 2.2), vandalism (2.3 to 0.8), and crimes against the person (0.67 to 0.8). The before and after periods consisted of six quarters or 18 months and 5 quarters or 15 months, respectively.

c   The figures in parentheses reflect the "value of goods lost expressed as a percentage of all goods sold" (Beck and Willis, 1999, p. 257).

Notes: Locations were in the UK unless otherwise specified; E = experimental area; C = control area; n.a. = not available; A&E = accident and emergency department; NS = non-significant.

3. Results

This chapter discusses the results of the 22 included CCTV evaluations. It also summarises key features of the evaluations which are important in the assessment of programme effects (e.g., other interventions, sample size, follow-up periods). The evaluations have been organised according to the setting in which the intervention took place. Three main settings were delineated: (1) city centre or public housing, (2) public transport, and (3) car parks.

City centre or public housing

Thirteen evaluations were identified that met the methodological criteria for inclusion in this review and assessed the impact of CCTV on crime in the setting of a city centre (N=11) or public housing (N=2). Three of the evaluations are reported in Mazerolle *et al.* (2000). Of the three settings, this contains the largest number of evaluations. Selected evaluations are discussed below and see Table 3.1 for summary information on each of the 13 evaluations.

Seven of the 13 evaluations were carried out in England, five in the U.S., and one in Scotland. On average, the duration of the follow-up evaluations was 10.9 months, ranging from a low of three months in the evaluation by Musheno *et al.* (1978) to a high of 24 months in the evaluations by Short and Ditton (1995) and Skinns (1998b). Only one of the evaluations (Skinns, 1998a) included other interventions in addition to the main intervention of CCTV. Many of the evaluations used multiple experimental areas (e.g., police beats, apartment buildings), meaning that the coverage of the CCTV intervention was quite extensive in the city or town centre. Multiple control areas (e.g., adjacent police beats, remainder of city) were also used by some of the evaluations.

As shown in Table 3.1, the city centre or public housing CCTV evaluations showed mixed results in their effectiveness in reducing crime. Five of the 13 evaluations were considered to have a desirable effect on crime, while three were considered to have an undesirable effect (increased crime). The remaining five evaluations were considered to have a null (clear evidence of no effect; N=4) or uncertain (unclear evidence of an effect; N=1) effect on crime.

Two evaluations of city centre CCTV schemes were conducted by Brown (1995). The first evaluation took place in Newcastle-upon-Tyne and involved the installation of 14 CCTV cameras in four police beats in the city centre (the experimental area). The control area comprised the seven remaining police beats of the city centre, which surrounded the experimental area. It is important to note that two cameras were installed in police beats which were part of the control area.

Fifteen months after the start of the programme, the monthly average of total crimes was reduced by 21.6 per cent (from 343 to 269) in the experimental area and 29.7 per cent (from 676 to 475) in the control area, which overall was an undesirable effect of CCTV. The measure of total crimes includes burglary, criminal damage, theft of vehicles, theft from vehicles, theft other, and juvenile disorder. Table 3.1 presents the results of the intervention for a number of these crimes. Reductions were observed in burglary, theft of vehicles, and theft from vehicles in both the experimental and control areas, with the reductions in the experimental area outpacing those in the control area. However, the number of these crimes in the experimental area was small. For example, burglary was reduced by 57.5 per cent in the experimental area (from 40 to 17) and 38.7 per cent in the control area (from 75 to 46). Brown (1995) found little evidence of territorial or functional (change in type of crime) displacement, but did find some evidence of diffusion of benefits, particularly for the crimes of burglary and criminal damage.

The second evaluation by Brown (1995) was carried out in Birmingham. In this programme, 14 CCTV cameras were installed in the centre of the city, with the cameras covering for the most part "shopping streets and partially open market areas", as well as some of the financial district. Three control areas were established, with streets in control area 1 (C1) receiving partial coverage by the CCTV system (see Table 3.1). Therefore, the experimental area was compared with control areas 2 and 3 combined.

After 12 months, total crimes, according to victim survey reports, were reduced in the experimental area, while total crimes increased in each of the three control areas. The actual number of crimes was much greater in the experimental area than in any of the control areas. Some evidence of what appears to be functional displacement (change in type of crime) was found, with offenders switching from robbery and theft from the person to theft from vehicles.

In the programme evaluated by Sarno (1995), 11 CCTV cameras were installed in the town centre of the London Borough of Sutton as part of the Safer Sutton Initiative launched in the early 1990s. The remaining part of the police sector in the town centre, which did not

Table 3.1: CCTV Evaluations in City Centres or Public Housing

Author, Publication Date, and Location	Context of Intervention	Type and Duration of Intervention	Sample Size	Other Interventions	Outcome Measure of Interest and Data Source	Research Design and Before-After Time Period	Results
Musheno, Levine, and Palumbo (1978), Bronxdale Houses, New York City, USA	Public housing	CCTV monitoring system (cameras in lobby and elevators; monitors in apartments); 3 months	E=3 buildings, C=3 buildings Note: project had 26 high-rises; 53 apartments in each	None	Crime (multiple offences); victim survey	Before-after, experimental-control Before=3 months; After=3 months	E vs C: total crimes: -9.4% (32 to 29) vs -19.2% (26 to 21) (uncertain effect)
1. Brown (1995), Newcastle-upon-Tyne centre	City or town	CCTV; 15 months	E=4 beats of central area, C=7 remaining beats of city centre Note: There are 2 other C, but each is less comparable to E	None Note: 14 of 16 cameras are in E; remaining 2 are in C	Crime (multiple offences); police records	Before-after, experimental control Before=26 months; After=15 months	E vs C (monthly average): total crimes: -21.6% (343 to 269) vs -29.7% (676 to 475); burglary: -57.5% (40 to 17, $p<.05$) vs -38.7% (75 to 46, $p<.05$); theft of vehicles: 47.1% (17 to 9, $p<.05$) vs -40.5% (168 to 100, $p<.05$); theft from vehicles: -50.0%

Study	Setting	Intervention	Conditions	Displacement	Outcome measures	Research design	Follow-up	Results
2. Brown (1995), Birmingham	City or town centre	CCTV; 12 months	E=Area 1 (streets with good coverage), C1=Area 2 (streets with partial coverage), C2=Area 4 (other streets in Zone A of Div. F), C3=Area 5 (streets in Zones B-G of Div. F)	None	Crime (total and most serious offences); victim survey	Before-after, experimental control	Before=12 months; After=12 months	(18 to 9, $p<.05$) vs -38.9% (106 to 65, $p<.05$) (undesirable effect) E vs C1: total crimes: -4.3% (163 to 156) vs +131.6% (19 to 44) E vs C2: total crimes: -4.3% vs +130.8% (26 to 60) E vs C3: total crimes: -4.3% vs +45.5% (33 to 48) (desirable effect)
Sarno (1995, 1996), London Borough of Sutton	Town centre	CCTV; 12 months	E=part of Sutton town centre, C1=rest of Sutton town centre, C2=all of Borough of Sutton	None	Crime (total and selected offences); police records	Before-after, experimental control	Before=12 months; After=12 months	E vs C1: total crimes (not including vehicle crime): -12.8% (1,655 to 1,443) vs -18% (data n.a.) E vs C2: total crimes: -12.8% vs -30% (data n.a.) (undesirable effect)

Short and Ditton (1995, 1996) and Ditton and Short (1998, 1999), Airdrie	Town centre	CCTV; 24 months	E=6 police beats, C1= rest of 6 police beats (not in camera vision), C2= rest of police sub-division, C3= rest of police division	None	Crime (total and multiple categories); police records	Before-after, experimental control; Before=24 months; After=24 months	E vs C3: total crimes: -35% (data n.a.) vs -12% (data n.a.) (desirable effect) Note: Data not provided to allow for comparisons of E with C1 or C2
Skinns (1998a, b), Doncaster	Town centre	CCTV; 12 months	E=all or parts of streets in vision of cameras in commercial areas, C=commercial areas of 4 adjacent townships	'Help points' for public to contact CCTV control rooms	Crime (total and selected offences); police records	Before-after, experimental control; Before=24 months; After=24 months; Note: There were 2 Es and 6 Cs used. The C used here is because the author says it was the most comparable to E Note: This E has been used because it includes the other E	E vs C: total police-recorded crimes: -21.3% (5,832 to 4,591) vs +11.9% (1,789 to 2,002) (desirable effect)

Squires (1998a), Ilford	Town centre	CCTV; 7 months	None	E=town centre, C=areas adjacent to town centre	Crime (total, violent, and selected offences); police records	Before-after, experimental-control. Before=6 months; After=7 months Note: 2 other Cs used, but less likely to be comparable to E	E vs C: total crimes: -17% (data n.a.) vs +9% (data n.a.) (desirable effect)
Armitage, Smyth, and Pease (1999), Burnley	Town centre	CCTV; 20 months	None	E=police beats with CCTV, C1=beats having a common boundary with CCTV beats, C2=other beats in police division	Crime (total and multiple offences); police records	Before-after, experimental-control. Before=12 months; After=12 months[a]	E vs C1: total crimes: -28% (1,805 to 1,410) vs -1% (6,242 to 6,180); violence: -35% (117 to 87) vs -20% (267 to 223); vehicle crimes: -48% (375 to 253) vs -8% (1,842 to 1,706); burglary: -41% (143 to 101) vs +9% (2,208 to 2,426) E vs C2: total crimes: -28% vs +9% (1,069 to 1,175); violence: -35% vs 0% (32 to 32); vehicle crimes:

| 1. Mazerolle, Hurley, and Chamlin (2000), Cincinnati (Northside), USA | City centre | CCTV; 3 months | E=1 site with CCTV, C= 1,000 foot radius BZ | None | Calls for service (weekly average); police records | Before-after, experimental-control

Before=23 months; After=6 months
Note: 2 other Cs of 200 and 500 foot radii were used and are included in the 1,000 foot radius C | -48% vs -8% (309 to 285); burglary: -41% vs +34% (366 to 555) (desirable effect)

E vs C (weekly average): +1.8% (901 to 917) vs 0% (36 to 36); (null effect) |
| 2. Mazerolle, Hurley, and Chamlin (2000), Cincinnati (Hopkins Park), USA | City centre/park | CCTV; 3 months | E=1 site with CCTV, C= 1,000 foot radius BZ | None | Calls for service (weekly average); police records | Before-after, experimental-control

Before=23 months; After=4 months
Note: 2 other Cs of 200 and 500 foot radii were used and are included in the 1,000 foot radius C | E vs C (weekly average): +9.8% (1,062 to 1,166) (vs 0% (22 to 22); (null effect) |

	Context	Intervention	Sample	Displacement	Outcome measure	Research design	Results
3. Mazerolle, Hurley, and Chamlin (2000), Cincinnati (Findlay Market), USA	City centre	CCTV; 2 months	E=1 site with CCTV, C= 1,000 foot radius BZ	None	Calls for service (weekly average); police records	Before-after, experimental-control Before=24.5 months; After=3.5 months Note: 2 other Cs of 200 and 500 foot radii were used and are included in the 1,000 foot radius C	E vs C (weekly average): +16.9% (1,005 to 1,175) vs +17.1% (111 to 130) (null effect)
Williamson and McLafferty (2000), Brooklyn, New York, USA	Public housing	CCTV; 18 months	E=9 buildings (1,220 apartments; Albany project), C=no. of buildings n.a. (Roosevelt project)	None	Crime (total and multiple categories) inside housing projects and inside zones of 0.1 to 0.5 miles radii around projects; police records	Before-after, experimental-control with matching Before=18 months; After=18 months	E vs C: change in total crimes inside projects: 0% vs -5.3%; change in total crimes inside 0.1 mile BZ: 0% vs -4.0%; change in major felonies inside projects: -22.8% vs -14.5%; change in major felonies inside 0.1 mile BZ: -6.4% vs -8.6% (data n.a.) (null effect)

Farrington, Bennett, and Welsh (2002), Cambridge	City centre	CCTV; 11 months	E=city centre, C = secondary centre	None	Crime (total and multiple categories); police records Also victim survey data on crime and disorder	Before-after, experimental-control Before=11 months; After=11 months	E vs C: total crimes: -13.8% (2,600 to 2,242) vs -26.9% (1,324 to 968); violent crimes: -6.0% (151 to 142) vs -33.8% (77 to 51); vehicle crimes: -53.1% (224 to 105) vs -54.0% (250 to 115); percentage victimized: +8.0% (26.4% to 28.5%) vs +19.3% (11.4% to 13.6%) (undesirable effect)

a   There was an additional eight months of follow-up, but the authors reported crime data as percentage changes relative to the 12-month before period, so it was not possible accurately to calculate the number of incidents for the additional eight months.

Notes: Locations were in the UK unless otherwise specified; BZ = buffer zone (area surrounding experimental area); E = experimental area; C = control area; n.a. = not available.

21

receive any CCTV coverage, served as the control area. (One other control area was used, but it was not comparable to the experimental area.) Twelve months after the programme began, total police-recorded crime (not including vehicle crime) had decreased by 12.8 per cent in the experimental area but by 18 per cent in the control area. Sarno did not investigate the possibility of displacement or diffusion of benefits.

Short and Ditton (1995) evaluated a CCTV scheme in Airdrie town centre, which involved 12 cameras spread over six police beats; this comprised the experimental area, and the comparable control area was the remainder of the six police beats not in camera vision. (Two other control areas were used, but the only data supplied was for the rest of the police division.) After 24 months, total police-recorded crime had decreased by 35 per cent in the experimental area compared with a 12 per cent decline in the control area. Short and Ditton found some evidence of diffusion of crime prevention benefits from the experimental area to the control area.

The programme evaluated by Skinns was a "multi-agency, police-led, town centre system, consisting of 63 cameras located in the commercial centre, multi-storey car parks and main town centre arterial roads" (1998a, p. 176). The programme has been included here, as opposed to in the setting of car parks, because the main focus of the intervention was the town centre. As noted above, another intervention was used: "help points" were established within the experimental area to aid the public in contacting the main CCTV control room. The experimental area included all or parts of streets in vision of the cameras. (Another experimental area was used but it is included in this experimental area.) The control area includes commercial areas of four adjacent townships. Five other control areas were used, but Skinns noted that these control areas were less comparable with the experimental area than the one used in this present report for experimental-control comparisons.

Twenty-four months after the start of the programme, total police-recorded crime had reduced in the experimental area by 21.3 per cent, but it had increased in the control area by 11.9 per cent. The author found no evidence that total crimes were displaced from the experimental area to the control area. The increase in crime in the control area was judged by the author to be due to pre-existing trends.

In the programme evaluated by Squires (1998a), an unknown number of CCTV cameras were installed in Ilford town centre to address a range of crime problems; areas adjacent to the town centre served as the control condition. (Two other control areas were used, but their comparability with the experimental area is less likely.) Seven months after the programme began, total police-recorded crime had fallen by 17 per cent in the experimental area, but had increased by 9 per cent in the control area. Squires found some evidence that crimes, particularly robbery and residential burglary, had been displaced from the town centre to adjacent areas (the control area).

In the programme evaluated by Armitage and her colleagues (1999), an unknown number of cameras were installed in the town centre of Burnley. The experimental area consisted of police beats in the town centre with CCTV coverage. Two control areas were used. The first comprised those police beats which shared a common boundary with the beats covered by CCTV. The second control area consisted of other police beats in the police division. The first control area was more comparable to the experimental area.

After 12 months, the experimental area, compared with the two control areas, showed substantial reductions in violent crime, burglary, vehicle crime, and total crime (see Table 3.1). For example, total incidents of crime fell by 28 per cent (from 1,805 to 1,410) in the experimental area compared with a slight decline of one per cent (from 6,242 to 6,180) in control area 1 and an increase of nine per cent (from 1,069 to 1,175) in control area 2. The authors found evidence of diffusion of benefits for the categories of total crime, violent crime, and vehicle crime, and evidence of territorial displacement for burglary.

In the three Cincinnati programmes by Mazerolle et al. (2000) the outcome measure used to evaluate the impact on crime was (weekly average) calls for police service, and the evaluation included one experimental and three control areas, the latter being "buffer zones" of varying distances around the experimental area. The outcome measure was limited to total calls for police service. The authors also reported on police calls for disorder (disorderly persons, curfew violation, neighbour trouble, noise complaints, and suspicious persons or vehicles) and drugs for the three buffer zones, but not for the experimental site; therefore, comparisons could not be made between experimental and control sites for disorder and drug offences.

The impact of CCTV on calls for police service was fairly consistent across the three locations: calls for service increased in the experimental site and increased or remained the same in the three control sites or buffer zones. For the Findlay Market programme, crime also increased in the two farthest buffer zones (500 and 1,000 feet away). Overall, CCTV did not have a desirable effect on calls for service in the experimental sites of the three locations. All of these schemes had a null effect on crime. The authors investigated the possibility of displacement in the Northside and Findlay Market programmes. In Northside, the authors found little or no evidence of displacement, while in Findlay Market, the authors concluded that the "results tend to suggest some displacement of activity as reflected in calls for service" (Mazerolle et al., 2000, p. 24).

In the programme evaluated by Farrington *et al.* (2002), 30 cameras were installed in Cambridge City centre. The control area was a secondary city centre shopping area (the Grafton centre) where there were no cameras on the streets. Comparing 11 months after the cameras were installed with the comparable 11 month period before, police-recorded crimes had decreased by 13.9 per cent in the experimental area (from 2,600 to 2,242) but by 26.9 per cent in the control area (from 1,324 to 968). Hence, there was an undesirable effect of CCTV on police-recorded crimes. Violent crimes (assault and robbery) also decreased more in the control area, while vehicle crimes (theft of and from vehicles) decreased equally in the experimental and control areas. Interviews were also carried out with quota samples of persons in the areas before and after the CCTV installation, asking them about their victimization (insulted or bothered, threatened, assaulted, or mugged) in the previous 12 months. The percentage victimized increased from 26.4 per cent to 28.5 per cent in the experimental area and from 11.4 per cent to 13.6 per cent in the control area, suggesting that the installation of CCTV had no effect on victimization. These results suggested that CCTV may have had no effect on crime but may have caused increased reporting to and/or recording by the police.

Only two evaluations (Musheno *et al.*, 1978; Williamson and McLafferty, 2000) were identified that met the methodological criteria for inclusion in this review and assessed the impact of CCTV on crime in the setting of public housing. Both of the schemes took place in New York City, but were implemented many years apart: the former in 1976 and the latter in 1998. The research design of the evaluation by Williamson and McLafferty (2000) was particularly rigorous, employing matching techniques to control for pre-existing differences (i.e., size of the housing communities, demographics, and neighbourhood location) between the experimental and control areas. Concerning the research design of the other programme, Musheno *et al.* (1978) took efforts to make the respondents of the victim survey comparable in the experimental and control areas; for example, half of the residents of the three experimental (all apartments received the intervention) and three control buildings were randomly selected to participate in the survey, which was administered before and after the CCTV intervention.

Both of the programmes did not involve interventions other than CCTV, although the application of CCTV differed somewhat between the two evaluations. In the programme by Williamson and McLafferty, cameras were installed at various locations in the experimental project (e.g., all elevators, lobbies, and roofs of buildings, and common areas and building water tanks) and were monitored – from a remote location – 24 hours a day, seven days a week, by uniformed officers of the New York City Police Department. In the other programme, cameras were installed in all of the lobbies and elevators of the experimental buildings, but were monitored by the residents themselves: the cameras "transmit pictures continuously to every resident's television receiver ... The top half of the screen telecasts the lobby and the bottom half shows the inside of the elevator viewed from above. Sounds emitted in these locations are also communicated to tenants' sets" (Musheno et al., 1978, p. 648).

Another difference between the two evaluations is the scale of the intervention, for both the number of CCTV cameras installed and the number of experimental sites used. In the evaluation by Williamson and McLafferty, a total of 105 cameras were installed at nine buildings (the experimental project), comprising a total of more than 1,200 apartments; in the evaluation by Musheno et al., three buildings, comprising a total of just over 150 apartments, were used as the experimental site (see Table 3.1). The authors did not report the number of cameras used, but considering that cameras were only installed in the lobbies and elevators, it is likely that the numbers were quite low.

The evaluation by Musheno et al. showed that, three months after the cameras were installed, total incidents of crime were reduced in both the experimental and control sites: -9.4 per cent and -19.2 per cent, respectively. However, as illustrated in Table 3.1, the number of crimes recorded was very low. This has the effect of inflating the before-after percentage changes and limiting the examination of programme results to total crimes (the numbers for individual crime types are even smaller). Because of small numbers, it was concluded that this programme had an uncertain effect on crime. The authors did not investigate the possibility of displacement or diffusion of benefits, but it is likely that neither occurred.

Williamson and McLafferty evaluated the impact of the CCTV intervention 18 months after the start of the programme and focused on crime inside the public housing projects and inside "buffer zones" of 0.1 to 0.5 miles radii around the projects. (For the buffer zones, only results inside 0.1 mile are reported here, as the intervention is less likely to affect behaviour beyond this point.) The housing project that received the intervention did not show any change in the total number of police-recorded crimes, either inside the project or inside the 0.1 mile buffer zone, while total crime in the control project dropped by 5.3 per cent inside the project and 4.0 per cent inside the 0.1 mile buffer zone. When total crime is disaggregated, a desirable programme effect is observed for major felonies in both experimental and control projects (see Table 3.1). However, the authors noted that "the substantial decrease in major felonies around both public housing projects seems to be part of a larger downward trend that was occurring not only in Brooklyn but across New York City in the late 1990s" (Williamson and McLafferty, 2000, p. 7). The authors investigated the possibility of displacement and diffusion of benefits and concluded that there is "no clear evidence" of either, "as the change in crime around the two housing projects does not vary predictably with distance" (ibid., p. 7).

Table 3.2 presents the results of a meta-analysis of the CCTV evaluations in city centres or public housing. In order to carry out a meta-analysis, a comparable measure of effect size is needed in each project. This has to be based on the number of crimes in the experimental and control areas before and after the CCTV intervention, because this is the only information that is regularly provided in these evaluations. Here, the odds ratio is used as the measure of effect size. For example, in Doncaster, the odds of a crime after given a crime before in the control area were 2,002/1,780 or 1.12. The odds of a crime after given a crime before in the experimental area were 4,591/5,832 or 0.79. The odds ratio therefore was 1.12/0.79 or 1.42. This was statistically highly significant (z = 9.24, p<.0001).

The odds ratio has a very simple and meaningful interpretation. It indicates the proportional change in crime in the control area compared with the experimental area. In this example, the odds ratio of 1.42 indicates that crime increased by 42 per cent in the control area compared with the experimental area. An odds ratio of 1.42 could also indicate the crime decreased by 30 per cent in the experimental area compared with the control area, since the change in the experimental area compared with the control area is the inverse of the odds ratio, or 1/1.42 here.

The odds ratio could only be calculated for nine evaluations, because numbers of crimes were not reported in the Airdrie, Ilford, Brooklyn, or (for the control area) Sutton evaluations. It shows that CCTV had a significant effect on crime in five evaluations: three desirable (Birmingham, Doncaster, and Burnley) and two undesirable (Newcastle and Cambridge). CCTV had no effect on crime in the four North American evaluations (see Table 3.2).

Table 3.2: Meta-Analysis of CCTV Evaluations in City Centres or Public Housing

Evaluation	Odds Ratio
1. Musheno et al. (1978), New York City	0.89
2. Brown (1995), Newcastle-upon-Tyne	0.90 *
3. Brown (1995), Birmingham	1.91 *
4. Skinns (1998a), Doncaster	1.42 *
5. Armitage et al. (1999), Burnley	1.27 *
6. Mazerolle et al. (2000), Cincinnati (Northside)	0.98
7. Mazerolle et al. (2000), Cincinnati (Hopkins Park)	0.91
8. Mazerolle et al. (2000), Cincinnati (Findlay Market)	1.00
9. Farrington et al. (2002), Cambridge	0.85 *
ALL 9 STUDIES	1.02 *
5 UK STUDIES	1.04 *
4 USA STUDIES	0.98

*p<.05.

In order to produce a summary effect size in a meta-analysis, each effect size has to have a standard error. This was one reason for choosing the odds ratio, which has a known standard error. The average effect size (weighted according to the standard error of each study) was an odds ratio of 1.02, which was not statistically significant ($z = 1.40$, n.s.). Thus, pooling the data from the nine studies, there was no evidence that CCTV led to a reduction in crime.

The nine effect sizes were significantly variable ($Q = 164.9$, 8 df, p<.0001). This means that they were not randomly distributed about the average effect size. The four American studies showed a null effect on crime (OR = 0.98, $z = 0.79$, n.s.), and they were homogeneous ($Q = 0.62$, 3 df, n.s.). The five UK studies showed a small but significant effect on crime (OR = 1.04, $z = 2.51$, p = .012), but they were significantly heterogeneous ($Q = 157.5$, 4 df, p<.0001).

Public transport

Four evaluations were identified that met the methodological criteria for inclusion in this review and assessed the impact of CCTV on crime in public transportation systems. All of the evaluations were conducted in subway systems: three in the London Underground (Burrows, 1979; two by Webb and Laycock, 1992) and one in the Montreal Metro (Grandmaison and Tremblay, 1997).

With the exception of the programme by Grandmaison and Tremblay, all of the programmes involved interventions in addition to CCTV. In the programme by Burrows (1979), notices were posted to alert people to the presence of CCTV cameras and special police patrols were in operation prior to the installation of CCTV. (In the evaluation of this programme, Burrows controlled for the effect of the police patrols by using as the before period the 12 months prior to the patrols coming into operation. The police patrols were discontinued at the time the CCTV was implemented, so there was no direct influence of the patrols during the after period.) For the two other London Underground programmes, some of the other interventions that were used included: passenger alarms, kiosks to monitor CCTV, and mirrors (see Table 3.3). It is important to note that, in the two evaluations by Webb and Laycock, both involved the expansion rather than the introduction of CCTV. For each of these three Underground programmes, CCTV was, however, the main intervention.

In the first Underground CCTV experiment (Burrows, 1979), CCTV cameras were installed in four stations in the southern sector (the experimental area). Two control areas, which did not receive the CCTV intervention, were used: (1) the remaining 15 stations in the southern sector and (2) the other 228 Underground stations. Burrows noted that the first control area was the most comparable to the experimental area, because "[t]he risk of the robbery and to a lesser extent theft [from the person] was disproportionately high in the southern sector of the system" (1979, p. 23). Table 3.3 presents comparisons of the experimental area with both control areas and for both offences. As noted above, efforts were made to control for the influence of special police patrols that were in operation in the experimental area prior to the introduction of CCTV.

After 12 months, the programme showed a desirable effect on crime. Compared with the two control areas, the experimental area showed substantial reductions in robbery and theft. But as illustrated in Table 3.3, the number of incidents of robbery recorded by the British Transport Police (BTP) in the experimental and first control area were very low. Reductions in theft, on the other hand, appear to be more robust. Theft declined by 72.8 per cent (from 243 to 66) in the experimental area, compared with declines of 26.5 per cent (from 535 to 393) and 39.4 per cent (from 4,884 to 2,962) in the first and second control areas, respectively. Burrows investigated whether the intervention displaced thefts to other times (temporal displacement) and to other no-treatment area stations (territorial displacement). He ruled out temporal displacement, because the CCTV system "operated at all times", but he did find some evidence of territorial displacement: "comparison of crime levels between stations subject to CCTV and other nearby stations in the southern sector provides evidence that is consistent with (though not proof of) some displacement of theft offences" (Burrows, 1979, p. 27).

The two other Underground CCTV programmes evaluated by Webb and Laycock showed mixed results. In the first programme, CCTV cameras were installed in six stations on the south end of the northern line (experimental area). Again, two no-treatment control areas were used: (1) six stations on the north end of the northern line and (2) the 236 other Underground stations. (The total number of Underground stations was 248 here and 247 for Burrows.) It is important to note that the authors make no mention of the comparability of the experimental with the control areas, although, as in the evaluation by Burrows, it is likely that the experimental area is more comparable with the first control area than the second. However, a comparison with other stations in the southern sector would have been better.

The programme lasted for 26 months and at this time it was evaluated for its effect on robbery. The programme was effective. Robberies (BTP-recorded incidents per month) were reduced by 62.3 per cent in the experimental area (from 5.3 to 2.0), compared with

Table 3.3: CCTV Evaluations in Public Transport

Author, Publication Date, and Location	Context of Intervention	Type and Duration of Intervention	Sample Size	Other Interventions	Outcome Measure of Interest and Data Source	Research Design and Before- After Time Period	Results
Burrows (1979, 1980), "Underground", London	Public transport (subway)	CCTV; 12 months	E=4 stations on southern sector, C1=15 other stations on southern sector, C2=228 other Underground stations	Notices of CCTV (also special police patrols preceded CCTV)	Personal theft and robbery; BTP records	Before-after, experimental-control. Before=12 months; After=12 months	E vs C1: robbery: -22.2% (9 to 7) vs +23.1% (13 to 16); theft: -72.8% (243 to 66) vs -26.5% (535 to 393). E vs C2: robbery: -22.2% vs +116.3% (43 to 93); theft: -72.8% vs -39.4% (4,884 to 2,962) (desirable effect)
1. Webb and Laycock (1992), "Underground", London	Public transport (subway)	CCTV (expansion of); 26 months	E=6 stations on south end of Northern line, C1=6 stations on north end of line, C2=236 other Underground stations	Passenger alarms, visible kiosk to monitor CCTV, mirrors, and improved lighting	Robbery; BTP records	Before-after, experimental-control. Before=46 months; After=26 months. Note: special policing used in E stations during first 3 years (1985-87) of before period	E vs C1 (monthly average): -62.3% (5.3 to 2.0) vs -50.0% (7.8 to 3.9). E vs C2: -62.3% vs -12.2% (69.6 to 61.1) (desirable effect). Note: for C2, Guardian Angels

29

	Setting	CCTV		Intervention	Outcome measure	Research design	Results
2. Webb and Laycock (1992), Oxford Circus station, "Underground", London	Public transport (subway)	CCTV (expansion of), 32 months	E=1 station, C=1 station	Passenger alarms, visible kiosk to monitor CCTV, and BTP patrols	Personal theft, robbery, and assault; BTP records	Before-after, experimental-control; Before= 28 months; After=32 months; (i.e., first 36 of 46 months of before period); in 1988 (remaining 10 months of before period), policing activity reduced in E stations; patrols began in May 1989 (7 months into 26 months of after period)	E vs C (monthly average): robbery: +47.1% (1.7 to 2.5) vs +21.4%; theft: +11.0% (31.0 to 34.4) vs -1.9% (20.8 to 20.4); assault: +29.4% (1.7 to 2.2) vs +36.4% (1.1 to 1.5) (undesirable effect)
Grandmaison and Tremblay (1997), "Metro", Montreal, Canada	Public transport (subway)	CCTV; 18 months	E=13 stations, C=52 stations	None	Crime (total and multiple offences); police records	Before-after, experimental-control with statistical analyses; Before=18 months; After=18 months	E vs C: total crimes: -20.0% (905 to 724) vs -18.3% (1,376 to 1,124); robbery: -27.0% (141 to 103) vs -30.8% (312 to 216); assault: -27.5% (178 to 129) vs +5.6% (233 to 246); total

theft and fraud:
-15.5% (388 to
328) vs -16.0%
(507 to 426)
(null effect)

Notes: Locations were in the UK unless otherwise specified; BTP = British Transport Police; E = experimental area; C = control area.

reductions of 50.0 per cent (from 7.8 to 3.9) and 12.2 per cent (from 69.6 to 61.1) in control areas 1 and 2, respectively. The authors found no evidence of robberies being displaced to the two groupings of control stations or a third grouping (nine other stations at the south end of the Northern and Victoria lines) that did not receive the intervention. Although not stated by the authors in such terms, evidence of diffusion of benefits is apparent.

The multiple interventions that were implemented in the experimental and control stations both before and after the start of the programme, including special police and Guardian Angels patrols (see Table 3.3), make it difficult to isolate the effect of CCTV, if any, on robbery. On this matter, the words of the authors are instructive:

> it seems likely that robbery has been kept down by improved management and staffing of the system, including more revenue protection as well as station staff. The policing changes may also have been helpful. It is also possible that the substantial physical work involved in station modernisation and the introduction of automatic ticket barriers in central area stations contributed by creating the impression of a more controlled and safer environment. (Webb and Laycock, 1992, p. 11)

The second Underground CCTV scheme evaluated by Webb and Laycock (1992) took place in Oxford Circus station located in central London. As noted above, this scheme did not just involve the expansion of CCTV, but also included other interventions: passenger alarms, visible kiosks to monitor CCTV operations, and patrols by the BTP. One station (Tottenham Court Road) that did not receive CCTV cameras was used as the control station. The scheme was evaluated after it had been in operation for 32 months.

Disappointing results were reported for the programme's effects on passenger robbery, theft (from the person), and assault. The authors noted that the robbery data were more reliable than the data on theft; no mention was made of the reliability of the assault data. Table 3.3 presents the results for before-after comparisons between the experimental and control stations for all three offences. After 32 months, the monthly incidence of robberies increased by almost half (47.1 per cent; from 1.7 to 2.5) in the experimental station, compared with an increase of more than one-fifth (21.4 per cent; from 1.4 to 1.7) in the control station. The programme's impact on theft was also undesirable. The authors did not investigate the possibility of displacement.

In the Montreal subway programme (Grandmaison and Tremblay, 1997), CCTV cameras were installed in 13 stations (approximately ten cameras per station) over the course of 18 months in the early 1990s. Fifty-two stations served as the control group. The programme was evaluated after 18 months of operation, and statistical analyses were conducted to control for past crime trends in the experimental and control stations.

Grandmaison and Tremblay found an equal reduction in (police-recorded) crime in both the experimental and control subway (Montreal Metro) stations: -20.0 per cent and -18.3 per cent, respectively. Hence, there was little evidence of any effect of the CCTV intervention. The measure of total crime included robbery, assault, purse snatching, other theft and fraud, vandalism, and other offences. From 18 months before the start of the intervention to 18 months afterwards, all categories of crimes were down in the experimental stations, while all categories except assault decreased in the control stations. The authors did not investigate the possibility of displacement or diffusion of benefits.

Overall, CCTV programmes in public transportation systems present conflicting evidence of effectiveness: two had a desirable effect, one had no effect, and one had an undesirable effect on crime. However, for the two effective programmes in the London Underground, the use of other interventions makes it difficult to say with certainty that CCTV produced the observed crime reductions, although in the programme by Burrows (1979) CCTV was more than likely the cause.

Table 3.4 shows the results of a meta-analysis of the CCTV evaluations in public transport settings. In all cases, the most comparable control area is used. The odds ratio was significant only in one case: the evaluation by Burrows (OR = 2.58, z = 6.39, p<.0001). When all four odds ratios were combined, the overall odds ratio was 1.06 (z = 1.37, n.s.), corresponding to a six per cent reduction in crimes in experimental areas compared with control areas.

Table 3.4: **Meta-Analysis of CCTV Evaluations in Public Transport or Car Parks**

Evaluation	Odds Ratio
Public Transport	
1. Burrows (1979), Underground	2.58 *
2. Webb and Laycock (1992), Underground	1.32
3. Webb and Laycock (1992), Underground (Oxford Circus)	0.89
4. Grandmaison and Tremblay (1997), Montreal	1.02
ALL 4 STUDIES	1.06
Car Parks	
1. Poyner (1991), Guildford	0.23
2. Tilley (1993b), Hartlepool	1.78 *
3. Tilley (1993b), Bradford	2.67 *
4. Tilley (1993b), Coventry	1.95 *
5. Sarno (1995), Sutton	1.49 *
ALL 5 STUDIES	1.70 *
ALL 18 STUDIES	1.04 *

*$p<.05$.

All four of these evaluations provided information about the effects of CCTV on violent crimes, but the numbers of violent crimes afterwards were very small in the evaluation by Burrows (1979). The Cambridge and Burnley evaluations in Table 3.1 also provided information on violent crimes. Combining these five evaluations (excluding the Burrows study), the overall odds ratio for the effect of CCTV on violent crimes was 0.96 ($z = 0.59$, n.s.), meaning that CCTV had no effect on violent crimes.

Car parks

We identified five CCTV evaluations that met the criteria for inclusion and were conducted in car parks or parking lots. All of the programmes were implemented in England between the early 1980s and the mid-1990s. The duration of the programmes ranged from a low of ten months to a high of 24 months (see Table 3.5). All of the programmes supplemented CCTV with other interventions, such as improved lighting, painting, fencing, payment schemes, notices about CCTV, and security personnel. In each programme, however, CCTV was the main intervention.

Table 3.5: CCTV Evaluations in Car Parks

Author, Publication Date, and Location	Context of Intervention	Type and Duration of Intervention	Sample Size	Other Interventions	Outcome Measure of Interest and Data Source	Research Design and Before-After Time Period	Results
Poyner (1991), University of Surrey, Guildford	Parking lot	CCTV; 10 months	E=1 parking lot (no. 4), C=1 parking lot (no. 1)	Improved lighting and foliage cut back (for both E and C; only E received CCTV)	Theft from vehicles; private security records	Before-after, experimental-control	E vs C (monthly average): theft from vehicles: -73.3% (3.0 to 0.8) vs -93.8% (1.6 to 0.1) (undesirable effect)
						Before=24 months; After=10 months	
1. Tilley (1993b), Hartlepool	Car park	CCTV; 24 months	E=CCTV covered car parks, C= non-CCTV covered car parks Note: no. of E and C car parks or spaces n.a.	Security officers, notices of CCTV, and payment scheme	Theft of and from vehicles; police records	Before-after, experimental-control	E vs C: theft of vehicles: -59.0% (21.2 to 8.7 per quarter year) vs -16.3% (16.0 to 13.4 per quarter year); theft from vehicles: -9.4% (6.4 to 5.8 per quarter year) vs +3.1% (16.0 to 16.5 per quarter year) (desirable effect)
						Before=15 months; After=30 months	
2. Tilley (1993b), Bradford	Car park	CCTV; 12 months	E=1 car park, C1=2 adjacent car park	Notices of CCTV, improved	Theft of and from vehicles; police records	Before-after, experimental control	E vs C1: theft of vehicles: -43.5% (23 to 13) vs

35

			parks, C2= adjacent street parking	lighting, and painting Note: C1 received some CCTV coverage for last 4 months		Before=12 months After=12 months Note: a third C is used, but is less comparable than C1 or C2		+5.9% (17 to 18); theft from vehicles: -68.8% (32 to 10) vs +4.5% (22 to 23) E vs C2: theft of vehicles: -43.5% vs +31.8% (22 to 29); theft from vehicles: -68.8% vs +6.1% (33 to 35) (desirable effect)
3. Tilley (1993b), Coventry	Car park	CCTV; various	E=3 car parks (BAR, BON, WHI), C=2 car parks (FAI, GRE)	Lighting, painting, and fencing	Theft of and from vehicles; police records	Before-after, experimental-control	Before and after = 8 months (E) and 16 months (C)	E vs C: theft of vehicles: -50.5% (91 to 45) vs -53.6% (56 to 26); theft from vehicles: -64.4% (276 to 101) vs -10.7% (150 to 134) (desirable effect)
Sarno (1995, 1996), London Borough of Sutton	Car park	CCTV; 12 months	E=3 car parks in part of Sutton police sector, C1=rest of Sutton sector, C2=all of Borough of Sutton	Multiple (e.g., locking overnight, lighting)	Vehicle crime; police records	Before-after, experimental-control	Before=12 months After=12 months	E vs C1: -57.3% (349 to 149) vs -36.5% (2,367 to 1,504) E vs C2: -57.3% vs -40.2% (6,346 to 3,798) (desirable effect)

Notes: All locations were in the UK; E = experimental area; C = control area; n.a. = not available.

Four of the programmes had a desirable effect and one had an undesirable effect on vehicle crimes, which was the exclusive focus of each of the impact evaluations. Poyner (1991) evaluated a multi-component scheme at the University of Surrey in Guildford in which both the experimental and control parking lots (one in each condition) received up-graded lighting and foliage was cut back, but only the experimental parking lot received CCTV. Ten months after the programme started, Poyner found that thefts from vehicles were substantially reduced in both the experimental and control parking lots. In the experimental site, the monthly average of incidents declined by almost three-quarters (73.3 per cent; from 3.0 to 0.8), while in the control site, they were almost eliminated (a drop of 93.8 per cent; from 1.6 to 0.1). Although the numbers are small, these results suggest that CCTV had undesirable effects on crime. However, the author concluded that there was evidence of diffusion of benefits.

Tilley (1993b) evaluated three CCTV programmes in car parks in the following cities: Hartlepool, Bradford, and Coventry. Each scheme was part of the Safer Cities Programme. In Hartlepool, CCTV cameras were installed in an unknown number of covered car parks and the control area included an unknown number of non-CCTV covered car parks. Security personnel, notices of CCTV, and payment schemes were also part of the package of measures employed to reduce vehicle crimes. Twenty-four months after the programme began, thefts of and from vehicles had been substantially reduced in the experimental compared with the control car parks (see Table 3.5). Tilley (1993b, p. 9) concluded that, "The marked relative advantage of CCTV covered parks in relation to theft of cars clearly declines over time and there are signs that the underlying local trends [an increase in car thefts] begin to be resumed". The author suggests that the displacement of vehicle thefts from covered to non-covered car parks may be partly responsible for this.

In Bradford, CCTV cameras were installed in one multi-story car park in the city centre. Notices of CCTV, improved lighting, and general improvements in the form of painting were also implemented in the car park. Two adjacent car parks and adjacent street parking served as the control areas. A third control area – a city centre sub-division – was also used by Tilley, but it is considered here to be less comparable than the other two with the experimental area, and thus has not been used in experimental-control comparisons. It is important to note that the first control area – two adjacent car parks – also received some CCTV coverage, for the last four months of the 12-month follow-up period. Twelve months into the programme, thefts of and from vehicles showed substantial reductions in the experimental area, while both crimes showed increases in the two control areas (see Table 3.5). Again, displacement was not measured, and numbers of crimes were small.

In the third car park CCTV scheme evaluated by Tilley (1993b), in Coventry, cameras were installed at different times in five car parks, and not in a sixth. Yearly data for thefts of and from vehicles (for January to August) were presented for six years (1987-1992). Three car parks (Barracks, Bond Street, Whitefriars) were designated as experimental car parks, because crime data were available for at least one year before and one year after the installation of cameras. Two car parks were designated as control car parks, either because cameras were not installed in them (Fairfax Street) or because the cameras were only installed in the last year (Greyfriars). For the control car parks, crime data in the two years before the average year of CCTV installation (1989) were compared with crime data in the two years afterwards. The sixth car park (Cox Street) was not included in the analyses because cameras were installed in it in the first year. There were other (lighting, painting and fencing) improvements in these car parks during this time period. It was found that theft from vehicles decreased more in the experimental car parks, but theft of vehicles did not.

The most recent evaluation of the impact of CCTV on vehicle crime was carried out in the London Borough of Sutton (Sarno, 1995). CCTV cameras were installed in three car parks (experimental area) in one part of the Sutton police sector at high risk of vehicle crimes, and two control areas were established: (1) the remainder of the Sutton police sector and (2) all of the Borough of Sutton. The first control area was considered to be comparable to the experimental area.

The programme was evaluated after its first 12 months of operation. Total vehicle crimes ("theft of, theft from, criminal damage to, unauthorised taking of vehicles and vehicle interference"; Sarno, 1995, p. 22) were reduced by 57.3 per cent (from 349 to 149) in the experimental area, but there were also lesser reductions in control areas 1 (36.5 per cent; from 2,367 to 1,504) and 2 (40.2 per cent; 6,346 to 3,798). The author did not measure diffusion of benefits.

Tilley (1993b) attempted to investigate mechanisms that may or may not have played a role in the success of CCTV in preventing vehicle crimes in car parks. However, his conclusions about mechanisms were almost all negative. For example, the true probability of being caught did not increase, offenders were not removed by being caught, CCTV images were insufficiently clear to identify offenders, there was little increase in car park usage following the installation of CCTV (so no convincing evidence of increased natural surveillance or of cautious drivers being attracted to these car parks), and rarely any effective deployment of security staff. So why did CCTV allegedly have any effect? Tilley's main suggestion was that CCTV had an effect when it was combined with other crime prevention measures, but this fails to address the problem of determining whether the effect was caused by CCTV or by these other measures. Tilley made little attempt to address threats to internal validity (Cook and Campbell, 1979; Shadish et al., 2002).

Table 3.4 shows the results of a meta-analysis of the five CCTV evaluations in car parks. In four cases, the odds ratios showed a significant and desirable effect of CCTV. In the other case (Poyner, 1991), the effect was undesirable, but the small numbers meant that the odds ratio was not significant ($z = 1.35$). When all five odds ratios were combined, the overall odds ratio was 1.70 ($z = 7.45$, p<.0001). Thus, crime increased by 70 per cent in control areas compared with experimental areas, or conversely crime decreased by 41 per cent in experimental areas compared with control areas.

All five evaluations provided information about the effects of CCTV on vehicle crimes, as did the Cambridge, Newcastle and Burnley studies in Table 3.1. Combining these eight evaluations, the overall odds ratio for the effect of CCTV on vehicle crimes was 1.38 ($z = 7.63$, p<.0001). Thus, CCTV increased vehicle crimes by about 38 per cent in control areas compared with experimental areas, or conversely decreased vehicle crimes by about 28 per cent in experimental areas compared with control areas.

Pooled meta-analysis results

Figure 3.1 summarises the results of 17 studies in a "Forest" graph. (The Guildford results of Poyner 1991 could not be shown.) This shows the odds ratio for total crime measured in each study plus its 95 per cent confidence interval. The 17 studies are ordered according to magnitudes of their odds ratios. It can immediately be seen that just over half of the studies (9 out of 17) showed evidence of a desirable effect of CCTV on crime, with odds ratios of 1.27 or greater (from Burnley upwards). All nine studies were carried out in the United Kingdom. Conversely, the other nine studies (including Guildford) showed no evidence of any desirable effect of CCTV on crime, with odds ratios of 1.02 or less. All five North American studies were in this group. The overall odds ratio of 1.04 (95 per cent confidence interval 1.01-1.06, $z = 2.97$, p = .003) indicates a significant but small overall reduction of four per cent in the crime rate in these 18 studies.

The 18 CCTV evaluation studies were significantly heterogeneous in their effect sizes ($Q = 267.9$, df = 17, p<.0001). The five North American studies were homogeneous in showing no desirable effect (OR = 0.99, $Q = 0.33$, df = 4, n.s.). The 13 UK studies showed a desirable effect (OR = 1.07, 95 per cent confidence interval 1.04-1.11, $z = 4.42$, p<.0001), but they were significantly heterogeneous even within the three context categories of city centres/public housing, public transport, and car parks.

Figure 3.1: CCTV evaluations

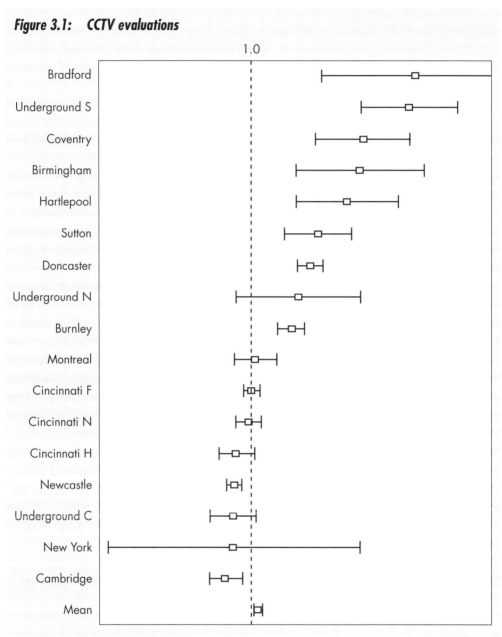

Note: Odds ratios and confidence intervals on logarithmic scale

4.   Conclusions

Summary of main findings

A number of targeted and comprehensive searches of the published and unpublished literature and contacts with leading researchers produced 22 CCTV evaluations which met our criteria for inclusion in this review; 24 evaluations did not meet the inclusion criteria (mainly because they had no comparable control condition) and were excluded. The criteria for inclusion called for CCTV programmes which employed rigorous evaluation designs to assess effects on crime, with the minimum design involving before-and-after measures of crime in experimental and comparable control areas.

Setting the threshold any higher – for example, requiring randomised experimental designs – was impractical, because no CCTV programme has been evaluated with this degree of scientific rigour. Therefore, the methodological criteria used here sought to achieve a balance between weak (e.g., simple one group, no control group, before-after designs) and strong science. Faced with a similar dilemma, Sherman and his colleagues adopted the same approach: "The report [Preventing Crime] takes the middle road between reaching very few conclusions with great certainty and reaching very many conclusions with very little certainty" (1998, p. 6).

The 22 included evaluations were carried out in three main settings: (1) city centres and public housing, (2) public transport, and (3) car parks. Evaluations were not evenly distributed across the three settings. The largest number of evaluations was in the city centre/public housing setting (N=13).

Of the 22 included evaluations, half (11) found a desirable effect on crime and five found an undesirable effect on crime. Five evaluations found a null effect on crime (i.e., clear evidence of no effect), while the remaining one was classified as finding an uncertain effect on crime (i.e., unclear evidence of an effect).

Results from a meta-analysis provide a clearer picture of the crime prevention effectiveness of CCTV. From 18 evaluations – the other four did not provide the needed data to be included in the meta-analysis – it was concluded that CCTV had a significant desirable effect on crime, although the overall reduction in crime was a rather small four per cent. Half of the studies (nine out of 18) showed evidence of a desirable effect of CCTV on crime.

All nine of these studies were carried out in the UK. Conversely, the other nine studies showed no evidence of any desirable effect of CCTV on crime. All five North American studies were in this group.

The meta-analysis also examined the effect of CCTV on the most frequently measured crime types. It was found that CCTV had no effect on violent crimes (from five studies), but had a significant desirable effect on vehicle crimes (from eight studies).

Across the three settings, mixed results were found for the crime prevention effectiveness of CCTV. In the city centre and public housing setting, there was evidence that CCTV led to a negligible reduction in crime of about two per cent in experimental areas compared with control areas. CCTV had a very small but significant effect on crime in the five UK evaluations in this setting (three desirable and two undesirable), but had no effect on crime in the four North American evaluations. More schemes showed evidence of diffusion of benefits than displacement.

The four evaluations of CCTV in public transportation systems present conflicting evidence of effectiveness: two found a desirable effect, one found no effect, and one found an undesirable effect on crime. For the two effective studies, the use of other interventions makes it difficult to say with certainty that CCTV produced the observed crime reductions. The pooled effect size for all four studies was desirable (a six per cent reduction in experimental areas compared with control areas), but non-significant. Only two of the studies measured diffusion of benefits or displacement and evidence was found for each.

In car parks, there was evidence that CCTV led to a statistically significant reduction in crime of about 41 per cent in experimental areas compared with control areas. However, for all of the studies in this setting other measures were in operation at the same time as CCTV. Most studies did not measure either diffusion of benefits or displacement.

Priorities for research

Advancing knowledge about the crime prevention benefits of CCTV programmes should begin with attention to the methodological rigour of the evaluation designs. The use of a comparable control area by all of the 22 included evaluations went a long way towards ruling out some of the major threats to internal validity, such as selection, maturation, history, and instrumentation (see Cook and Campbell, 1979; Shadish et al., 2002). The effect of CCTV on crime can also be investigated after controlling (e.g., in a regression equation) not only for prior crime but also for other community-level factors that influence crime, such as neighbourhood poverty and poor housing. Another possible research design is to match two areas and then to choose one at random to be the experimental area. Of course, several pairs of areas would be better than only one pair.

Also important in advancing knowledge about the effectiveness of CCTV in preventing crime is attention to methodological problems or changes to programmes that take place during and after implementation. Some of these implementation issues include: statistical conclusion validity (adequacy of statistical analyses), construct validity (fidelity), and statistical power (to detect change). For some of the included evaluations, small numbers of crimes made it difficult to determine whether or not the programme had an effect on crime. It is essential to carry out statistical power analyses before embarking on evaluation studies (Cohen, 1977). Few studies attempted to control for regression to the mean, which happens if an intervention is implemented just after an unusually high crime rate period. A long time series of observations is needed to investigate this. The contamination of control areas (i.e., by the CCTV intervention) was another, albeit less common, problem that faced the evaluations.

Beyond evaluation design and implementation issues, there is also the need for longer follow-up periods to see how far the effects persist. Of the 22 included schemes, four were in operation for six months or less prior to being evaluated. This is a very short time to assess a programme's impact on crime or any other outcome measure, and for these programmes the question can be asked: Was the intervention in place long enough to provide an accurate picture of its observed effects on crime? Ideally, time series designs are needed with a long series of crime rates in experimental and control conditions before and after the introduction of CCTV. In the situational crime prevention literature, brief follow-up periods are the norm, but "it is now recognized that more information is needed about the longer-term effects of situational prevention" (Clarke, 2001, p. 29). Ideally, the same time periods should be used in before and after measures of crime.

Research is also needed to help identify the active ingredients of effective CCTV programmes. One-third of the included programmes involved interventions in addition to CCTV, and this makes it difficult to isolate the independent effects of the different components, and interactional effects of CCTV in combination with other measures. Future experiments are needed which attempt to disentangle elements of effective programmes. Also, future experiments need to measure the intensity of the CCTV dose and the dose-response relationship, and need to include alternative methods of measuring crime (surveys as well as police records).

Research is also needed on the financial costs and benefits of CCTV programmes. We had hoped to be able to examine this issue, but it was not possible, because only one (Skinns, 1998a) of the 22 programmes presented data on financial costs and benefits or conducted a cost-benefit analysis. Skinns (1998b) found that the criminal justice costs saved from fewer prosecutions and sentences (the benefits) were greater than the costs of running the CCTV programme by more than three times, or a benefit-cost ratio of 3.5:1. Previous work (Welsh and Farrington, 1999, 2000) has shown that situational crime prevention generally is an economically efficient strategy in preventing crime. It is important to measure the cost-effectiveness of CCTV in preventing crime compared with other alternatives such as improved street lighting.

Policy implications

In Britain, CCTV is the single most heavily funded non-criminal justice crime prevention measure. Over the three year period of 1999 through 2001, the British government has made available £170 million for "CCTV schemes in town and city centres, car parks, crime hot-spots and residential areas" (Home Office Policing and Reducing Crime Unit, 2001, p. 8). In previous years (1996 through 1998), CCTV accounted for more than three-quarters of total spending on crime prevention by the Home Office (Koch, 1998, p. 49).

During this time there has been much debate about the effectiveness of CCTV in preventing crime and, hence, on the wisdom of devoting such large sums of money to one type of intervention. A key issue is how far funding for CCTV in Britain has been based on high quality scientific evidence demonstrating its efficacy in preventing crime. There is a concern that this funding has been based partly on a handful of apparently effective schemes that were usually evaluated using simple one group (no control group) before-after designs. These evaluations were conducted with varying degrees of competence (Armitage et al., 1999, p. 226) and varying degrees of professional independence from the Home Office (Ditton and Short, 1999, p. 202). Future funding of CCTV schemes should be based on high quality scientific evidence that shows the efficacy of CCTV in preventing crime.

This report's findings of the highest quality British CCTV evaluations provide some support, albeit with the advantage of hindsight, for government expenditure on CCTV initiatives. However, it was noteworthy that the poorly controlled (excluded) studies produced more desirable results than the better controlled (included) studies.

The studies included in the present review show that CCTV can be most effective in reducing crime in car parks. Exactly what the optimal circumstances are for effective use of CCTV schemes is not entirely clear at present, and needs to be established by future evaluation research. But it is interesting to note that the success of the CCTV schemes in car parks was limited to a reduction in vehicle crimes (the only crime type measured) and all five schemes included other interventions, such as improved lighting and notices about CCTV cameras. Conversely, the evaluations of CCTV schemes in city centres and public housing measured a much larger range of crime types and the schemes did not involve, with one exception, other interventions. These CCTV schemes, and those focused on public transport, had only a small effect on crime. Could it be that a package of interventions focused on a specific crime type is what made the CCTV-led schemes in car parks effective? The research evidence on the effectiveness of situational crime prevention in general is ripe with such examples (e.g., for the prevention of convenience store robbery, see Hunter and Jeffery, 1992).

Overall, it might be concluded that CCTV reduces crime to a small degree. In light of the successful results, future CCTV schemes should be carefully implemented in different settings and should employ high quality evaluation designs with long follow-up periods. They should also attempt to establish the causal mechanisms by which CCTV has any effect on crime, by interviewing potential offenders. In the end, an evidence-based approach to crime prevention which uses the highest level of science available offers the strongest formula for building a safer society.

Appendix 1:   Literature reviews consulted

The following five literature reviews were consulted as part of the search strategies used to identify evaluation reports on the effects of CCTV on crime.

Eck, J.E. (1997). Preventing crime at places. In L.W. Sherman, D.C. Gottfredson, D.L. MacKenzie, J.E. Eck, P. Reuter, and S.D. Bushway, *Preventing Crime: What Works, What Doesn't, What's Promising* (chapter 7). Washington, DC: National Institute of Justice, US Department of Justice.

Eck, J.E. (2002). Preventing crime at places. In L.W. Sherman, D.P. Farrington, B.C. Welsh, and D.L. MacKenzie (eds.), *Evidence-Based Crime Prevention* (241-94). London: Routledge.

Nieto, M. (1997). *Public Video Surveillance: Is It an Effective Crime Prevention Tool?* Sacramento, California: California Research Bureau, California State Library.

Phillips, C. (1999). A review of CCTV evaluations: Crime reduction effects and attitudes towards its use. In K. Painter and N. Tilley (eds.), *Surveillance of Public Space: CCTV, Street Lighting and Crime Prevention: Vol. 10. Crime Prevention Studies* (pp. 123-55). Monsey, NY: Criminal Justice Press.

Poyner, B. (1993). What works in crime prevention: An overview of evaluations. In R.V. Clarke (ed.), *Crime Prevention Studies: Vol. 1* (pp. 7-34). Monsey, NY: Criminal Justice Press.

Appendix 2: Evaluation reports that could not be obtained

The following three evaluation reports were identified, but we were not successful in obtaining copies. It is not known if these evaluations would meet the inclusion criteria.

Berkowitz, M. (1975). *Evaluation of Merchant Security Program: A Case Study Assessing the Impact of Electronic Protection Devices on Safety in Retail Stores in New York City*. New York: New York City Police Department.

James, S. and Wynne, R. (1985). *Tenant Perceptions of Crime and Security on Melbourne's High-Rise Housing Estates*. Melbourne, Australia: Criminology Department, University of Melbourne.

Northumbria Police (no date). *Car Crime – Let's Crack It Campaign*. Force evaluation, 1988. Northumbria: Author.

References

Armitage, R., Smyth, G., and Pease, K. (1999). Burnley CCTV evaluation. In K. Painter and N. Tilley (eds.), *Surveillance of Public Space: CCTV, Street Lighting and Crime Prevention: Vol. 10. Crime Prevention Studies (pp.* 225-50). Monsey, NY: Criminal Justice Press.

Barr, R. and Pease, K. (1990). Crime placement, displacement, and deflection. In M. Tonry and N. Morris (eds.), *Crime and Justice: A Review of Research: Vol. 12* (pp. 277-318). Chicago, Illinois: University of Chicago Press.

Beck, A. and Willis, A. (1999). Context-specific measures of CCTV effectiveness in the retail sector. In K. Painter and N. Tilley (eds.), *Surveillance of Public Space: CCTV, Street Lighting and Crime Prevention: Vol. 10. Crime Prevention Studies* (pp. 251-69). Monsey, NY: Criminal Justice Press.

Bromley, R. and Thomas, C. (1997). Vehicle crime in the city centre: Planning for secure parking. *Town Planning Review, 68,* 257-78.

Brown, B. (1995). *CCTV in Town Centres: Three Case Studies.* (Crime Detection and Prevention series paper 68.) London: Home Office.

Burrows, J.N. (1979). The impact of closed circuit television on crime in the London Underground. In P. Mayhew, R.V.G. Clarke, J.N. Burrows, J.M. Hough, and S.W.C. Winchester, *Crime in Public View* (pp. 21-29). (Home Office research study no. 49.) London: HMSO.

Burrows, J.N. (1980). Closed circuit television on the London Underground. In R.V.G. Clarke and P. Mayhew (eds.), *Designing Out Crime* (pp. 75-83). London: HMSO.

Burrows, J.N. (1991). *Making Crime Prevention Pay: Initiatives from Business.* (Crime Prevention Unit paper 27.) London: Home Office.

Carr, K. and Spring, G. (1993). Public transport safety: A community right and a communal responsibility. In R.V. Clarke (ed.), *Crime Prevention Studies: Vol. 1* (pp. 147-55). Monsey, NY: Criminal Justice Press.

Chatterton, M.R. and Frenz, S.J. (1994). Closed-circuit television: Its role in reducing burglaries and the fear of crime in sheltered accommodation for the elderly. *Security Journal, 5*, 133-39.

Clarke, R.V. (1995). Situational crime prevention. In M. Tonry and D.P. Farrington (eds.), *Building a Safer Society: Strategic Approaches to Crime Prevention: Vol. 19. Crime and Justice: A Review of Research* (pp. 91-150). Chicago, Illinois: University of Chicago Press.

Clarke, R.V. (2001). Effective crime prevention: Keeping pace with new developments. *Forum on Crime and Society, 1*, 17-33.

Clarke, R.V. and Homel, R. (1997). A revised classification of situational crime prevention techniques. In S.P. Lab (ed.), *Crime Prevention at a Crossroads* (pp. 17-27). Cincinnati, Ohio: Anderson.

Clarke, R.V. and Weisburd, D. (1994). Diffusion of crime control benefits: Observations on the reverse of displacement. In R.V. Clarke (Ed.), *Crime Prevention Studies: Vol. 2* (pp. 165-83). Monsey, NY: Criminal Justice Press.

Cohen, J. (1977). *Statistical Power Analysis for the Behavioral Sciences*. New York: Academic Press.

Cook, T.D. and Campbell, D.T. (1979). *Quasi-Experimentation: Design and Analysis Issues for Field Settings*. Chicago, Illinois: Rand McNally.

Davidson, J. and Farr, J. (1994). Mitchellhill Estate: Estate based management (concierge) initiative. In S. Osborn (ed.), *Housing Safe Communities: An Evaluation of Recent Initiatives* (pp. 22-33). London: Safe Neighbourhoods Unit.

Ditton, J. and Short, E. (1998). Evaluating Scotland's first town centre CCTV scheme. In C. Norris, J. Moran, and G. Armstrong (eds.), *Surveillance, Closed Circuit Television and Social Control* (pp. 155-73). Aldershot: Ashgate.

Ditton, J. and Short, E. (1999). Yes, it works, no, it doesn't: Comparing the effects of open-street CCTV in two adjacent Scottish town centres. In K. Painter and N. Tilley (eds.), *Surveillance of Public Space: CCTV, Street Lighting and Crime Prevention: Vol. 10. Crime Prevention Studies* (pp. 201-24). Monsey, NY: Criminal Justice Press.

Ditton, J., Short, E., Phillips, S., Norris, C., and Armstrong, G. (1999). *The Effect of Closed Circuit Television on Recorded Crime Rates and Public Concern About Crime in Glasgow.* Edinburgh: Central Research Unit, Scottish Office.

Eck, J.E. (1997). Preventing crime at places. In L.W. Sherman, D.C. Gottfredson, D.L. MacKenzie, J.E. Eck, P. Reuter, and S.D. Bushway, *Preventing Crime: What Works, What Doesn't, What's Promising* (chapter 7). Washington, DC: National Institute of Justice, US Department of Justice.

Eck, J.E. (2002). Preventing crime at places. In L.W. Sherman, D.P. Farrington, B.C. Welsh, and D.L. MacKenzie (eds.), *Evidence-Based Crime Prevention* (pp. 241-94). London: Routledge.

Farrington, D.P. (1983). Randomized experiments on crime and justice. In M. Tonry and N. Morris (eds.), *Crime and Justice: A Review of Research: Vol. 4* (pp. 257-308). Chicago, Illinois: University of Chicago Press.

Farrington, D.P. (1997). Evaluating a community crime prevention program. *Evaluation, 3,* 157-73.

Farrington, D.P., Bennett, T.H., and Welsh, B.C. (2002). Rigorous Evaluations of the Effects of CCTV on Crime. Unpublished manuscript. Cambridge: Institute of Criminology, University of Cambridge.

Farrington, D.P. and Petrosino, A. (2000). Systematic reviews of criminological interventions: The Campbell Collaboration Crime and Justice Group. *International Annals of Criminology, 38,* 49-66.

Farrington, D.P., Petrosino, A., and Welsh, B.C. (2001). Systematic reviews and cost-benefit analyses of correctional interventions. *Prison Journal, 81,* 339-59.

Farrington, D.P. and Welsh, B.C. (eds.). (2001). What Works in Preventing Crime? Systematic Reviews of Experimental and Quasi-Experimental Research [special issue]. *Annals of the American Academy of Political and Social Science, 578.*

Gill, M. and Turbin, V. (1998). CCTV and shop theft: Towards a realistic evaluation. In C. Norris, J. Moran, and G. Armstrong (eds.), *Surveillance, Closed Circuit Television and Social Control* (pp. 189-204). Aldershot: Ashgate.

Gill, M. and Turbin, V. (1999). Evaluating 'realistic evaluation': Evidence from a study of CCTV. In K. Painter and N. Tilley (eds.), *Surveillance of Public Space: CCTV, Street Lighting and Crime Prevention: Vol. 10. Crime Prevention Studies* (pp. 179-99). Monsey, NY: Criminal Justice Press.

Grandmaison, R. and Tremblay, P. (1997). Évaluation des effets de la télé-surveillance sur la criminalité commise dans 13 stations du Métro de Montréal. *Criminologie, 30,* 93-110.

Home Office Policing and Reducing Crime Unit (2001). Invitation to Tender: Evaluation of CCTV Initiatives. Unpublished document. London: Author.

Hunter, R.D. and Jeffery, C.R. (1992). Preventing convenience store robbery through environment design. In R.V. Clarke (ed.), *Situational Crime Prevention: Successful Case Studies* (pp. 194-204). Albany, NY: Harrow and Heston.

Johnson, B.R., De Li, S., Larson, D.B., and McCullough, M. (2000). A systematic review of the religiosity and delinquency literature: A research note. *Journal of Contemporary Criminal Justice, 16,* 32-52.

Koch, B.C.M. (1998). *The Politics of Crime Prevention.* Aldershot: Ashgate.

Mazerolle, L., Hurley, D.C., and Chamlin, M. (2000). *Social behavior in public space: An analysis of behavioral adaptations to CCTV.* Unpublished manuscript. Queensland, Australia: Griffith University.

Musheno, M.C., Levine, J.P., and Palumbo, D.J. (1978). Television surveillance and crime prevention: Evaluating an attempt to create defensible space in public housing. *Social Science Quarterly, 58,* 647-56.

National Association of Convenience Stores (November, 1991). *Convenience Store Security: Report and Recommendations.* Alexandria, VA: Author.

Nieto, M. (1997). *Public Video Surveillance: Is It an Effective Crime Prevention Tool?* Sacramento, California: California Research Bureau, California State Library.

Norris, C. and Armstrong, G. (1999). *The Maximum Surveillance Society: The Rise of CCTV.* Oxford: Berg.

Petrosino, A. (2000). Crime, drugs and alcohol. In *Contributions to the Cochrane Collaboration and the Campbell Collaboration: Evidence from Systematic Reviews of Research Relevant to Implementing the "Wider Public Health" Agenda*. NHS Centre for Reviews and Dissemination. http://www.york.ac.uk/inst/crd/wph.htm.

Petrosino, A., Turpin-Petrosino, C., and Finckenauer, J.O. (2000). Well-meaning programs can have harmful effects! Lessons from experiments of programs such as Scared Straight. *Crime and Delinquency, 46*, 354-79.

Phillips, C. (1999). A review of CCTV evaluations: Crime reduction effects and attitudes towards its use. In K. Painter and N. Tilley (eds.), *Surveillance of Public Space: CCTV, Street Lighting and Crime Prevention: Vol. 10. Crime Prevention Studies* (pp. 123-55). Monsey, NY: Criminal Justice Press.

Poyner, B. (1991). Situational crime prevention in two parking facilities. *Security Journal, 2*, 96-101.

Poyner, B. (1992). Video cameras and bus vandalism. In R.V. Clarke (ed.), *Situational Crime Prevention: Successful Case Studies* (pp. 185-93). Albany, NY: Harrow and Heston.

Reppetto, T.A. (1976). Crime prevention and the displacement phenomenon. *Crime and Delinquency, 22*, 166-77.

Sarno, C. (1995). Impact of CCTV on crime. In M. Bulos (ed.), *Towards a Safer Sutton? Impact of Closed Circuit Television on Sutton Town Centre* (pp. 4-32). London: London Borough of Sutton.

Sarno, C. (1996). The impact of closed circuit television on crime in Sutton town centre. In M. Bulos and D. Grant (eds.), *Towards a Safer Sutton? CCTV One Year On* (pp. 13-49). London: London Borough of Sutton.

Shadish, W.R., Cook, T.D., and Campbell, D.T. (2002). *Experimental and Quasi-Experimental Designs for Generalized Causal Inference*. Boston: Houghton Mifflin.

Sherman, L.W., Gottfredson, D.C., MacKenzie, D.L., Eck, J., Reuter, P., and Bushway, S.D. (1998). Preventing crime: What works, what doesn't, what's promising. *Research in Brief*, July. Washington, DC: National Institute of Justice, US Department of Justice.

Short, E. and Ditton, J. (1995). Does closed circuit television prevent crime? An evaluation of the use of CCTV surveillance cameras in Airdrie town centre. *Crime and Criminal Justice Research Findings, 8*. Edinburgh: Central Research Unit, Scottish Office.

Short, E. and Ditton, J. (1996). *Does Closed Circuit Television Prevent Crime? An Evaluation of the Use of CCTV Surveillance Cameras in Airdrie Town Centre*. Edinburgh: Central Research Unit, Scottish Office.

Sivarajasingam, V. and J.P. Shepherd (1999). Effect of closed circuit television on urban violence. *Journal of Accident and Emergency Medicine, 16*, 255-57.

Skinns, D. (1998a). Crime reduction, diffusion and displacement: Evaluating the effectiveness of CCTV. In C. Norris, J. Moran, and G. Armstrong (eds.), *Surveillance, Closed Circuit Television and Social Control* (pp. 175-88). Aldershot: Ashgate.

Skinns, D. (1998b). *Doncaster CCTV Surveillance System: Second Annual Report of the Independent Evaluation*. Doncaster: Faculty of Business and Professional Studies, Doncaster College.

Squires, P. (1998a). *An Evaluation of the Ilford Town Centre CCTV Scheme*. Brighton: Health and Social Policy Research Centre, University of Brighton.

Squires, P. (1998b). *CCTV and Crime Prevention in Burgess Hill Town Centre: An Independent Evaluation*. Brighton: Health and Social Policy Research Centre, University of Brighton.

Squires, P. (1998c). *CCTV and Crime Reduction in Crawley: An Independent Evaluation of the Crawley CCTV System*. Brighton: Health and Social Policy Research Centre, University of Brighton.

Squires, P. (1998d). *The East Grinstead Town Centre CCTV Scheme: An Independent Evaluation*. Brighton: Health and Social Policy Research Centre, University of Brighton.

Squires, P. and Measor, L. (1996). *CCTV Surveillance and Crime Prevention in Brighton: Follow-up Analysis*. Brighton: Health and Social Policy Research Centre, University of Brighton.

Taylor, G. (1999). Using repeat victimisation to counter commercial burglary: The Leicester experience. *Security Journal, 12*, 41-52.

Tilley, N. (1993a). *The Prevention of Crime Against Small Businesses: The Safer Cities Experience.* (Crime Prevention Unit series paper 45.) London: Home Office.

Tilley, N. (1993b). *Understanding Car Parks, Crime and CCTV: Evaluation Lessons from Safer Cities.* (Crime Prevention Unit series paper 42.) London: Home Office.

Webb, B. and Laycock, G. (1992). *Reducing Crime on the London Underground: An Evaluation of Three Pilot Projects.* (Crime Prevention Unit series paper 30.) London: Home Office.

Welsh, B.C. and Farrington, D.P. (1999). Value for money? A review of the costs and benefits of situational crime prevention. *British Journal of Criminology, 39,* 345-68.

Welsh, B.C. and Farrington, D.P. (2000). Monetary costs and benefits of crime prevention programs. In M. Tonry (ed.), *Crime and Justice: A Review of Research: Vol. 27* (pp. 305-61). Chicago, Illinois: University of Chicago Press.

Williamson, D. and McLafferty, S. (2000). The effects of CCTV on crime in public housing: An application of GIS and spatial statistics. Paper presented at the American Society of Criminology meeting, November 15-19, 2000, San Francisco, California.

RDS Publications

Requests for Publications

Copies of our publications and a list of those currently available may be obtained from:

Home Office
Research, Development and Statistics Directorate
Communication Development Unit
Room 275, Home Office
50 Queen Anne's Gate
London SW1H 9AT
Telephone: 020 7273 2084 (answerphone outside of office hours)
Facsimile: 020 7222 0211
E-mail: publications.rds@homeoffice.gsi.gov.uk

alternatively

why not visit the RDS web-site at
Internet: http://www.homeoffice.gov.uk/rds/index.htm

where many of our publications are available to be read on screen or downloaded for printing.